Looking for Someone to Care

The Reality of Love
In the Home of
The Foster Parent

Looking for Someone to Care

The Reality of Love
In the Home of
The Foster Parent

By

Ruth Thacker Fant

ISBN: 9781093841084
Independently published
April, 2019

DEDICATION

All Departments of Human Services in the US and Abroad.

All Child Protective Services in this great country of America.

Dedicated Social Workers and Caseworkers who are overworked and underrated.

The Great Foster Parents Resource: Parents, Forever Parents and Grandparents who are rearing grandchildren because of the drug epidemic.

To you and you; those who will become Super Stars of the FOSTER PARENTING COMMUNITY. You who have the talent and skills of parenting that you have not used... It's Discovery Time!

INTRODUCTION

Challenges present themselves on every hand, in every situation, especially and most of all in parenting. But as a child, can you imagine being removed from your home and parents and placed in the home of a total stranger?

Undertaking this process can prove to be extremely mentally challenging for a child. Yet, this process dictates the actions of the Department of Human Services (DHS) and Child Protective Services (CPS) all over the United States of America and in other countries. These services are vital, and of the utmost importance. The Departments of Human Services and Child Protective Services have an enormous job to do, and in my view, after Foster Parenting for twelve years, they do it painfully well.

Parenting has been put aside by the parents of the drug world who explore and experiment with opioids, crack cocaine, heroin, meth and many other drugs of choice. Human Services is the only way that a child who has been put aside and neglected, can experience caring, concern and love. We really should applaud these agencies. The training for foster parents is a total of three to four months.

The home must be safe and sanitary. The foster parent must be teachable and tolerant in order for these children to come into their homes with a wealth of insecurities.

The DHS agencies provide very good assistance for the child or children in scheduling them for psychological therapy. This has proven to be effective, and it is greatly needed in most situations. Motivating and channeling the foster child's interests and behavioral patterns is a somewhat complex encounter. This is where the hours of training come in. Also, your caseworker is there to assist you.

Maintaining a positive attitude is extremely essential to you and the child. This is where you find out you have patience that you, yourself, did not know about. Yes, this is the key to great foster parenting.

You will arrive, and in an enjoyable manner. These children are innocent victims of their environment. They are taught to steal and lie. There is a laundry list of negatives involved. The child does not understand why they are being removed from their parents, and their home. They tend to blame themselves. The therapy sessions are very helpful in turning around that negative thinking in the child.

At the end of the day, children still love their parents; therefore, agencies have an all-important reunification program that is so wonderful, because parents are given the opportunity to change and be given another chance. This is upon court approval.

There are so many amazing occurrences in foster parenting. I watched as a seven year old cried all the time while doing his homework. Within about a year he was doing his homework all by himself.

Another child who needed someone to sit with him in class (Wrap-Around Program) so he could concentrate, became an honor-roll student in about two years. Hope Springs Eternal!

Parenting is a challenge all by itself. One does not need drugs or anything else to make it more difficult. Learning experiences and teachable moments come to us in many forms, through people, places and things. I, as a foster parent of twelve years, had a challenging journey. It was quite a learning experience, and one that I enjoyed. Oh, yes! There were moments I wanted to give it all up, and one of those beautiful disenfranchised children would make me laugh by doing something unexpectedly positive.

There is a program that most of the foster agencies have where the foster parent can become the legal guardian. The child resides in the home until the age of eighteen years of age. This program requires additional training and microscopic viewing by the agency. This process is finalized by the court, and the end result is that the foster child becomes a legal member of the family.

Become a challenged individual by giving a victimized child the comforts of a loving home. You will be amazed at the level you will find in yourself; the understanding and patience that you possess. I came to understand why I was tearful when one of my boys was reunified with his mother. He calls me from time to time. He has graduated College and is a positive contributor to society. Hope really does spring eternal.

Buy the book. Enjoy the book. When you do I will be able to make some meaningful donations to organizations and non-profits that have programs for young people fifteen and older who came out of foster care. Some are homeless and some resorted to crime. You can buy the book as a gift – Christmas, birthday, or for any reason. Enjoy. I do thank you.

Sincerely,
Ruth Thacker Fant

A CHILD IS AMAZING

★

A child's laughter can make
an angel sing.

A child's innocence creates an
aura of wisdom.

A child's smile can warm the
heart beyond measure.

A child's hands are the
potential artists of the world.

A child's hope can illuminate
the Promise of God.

A child's strength can move
the highest mountain.

A child's love can create the
most beautiful universe.

A child's concept can put an
adult on notice.

A child's peace can be found
in a sea of turmoil.

A child's understanding can
be the anchor for a large ship.

A child's talents and gifts
show they are given by God.

A child's tolerance can be
magical.

A child's wisdom is an
unbelievable protection.

A child's resilience transcends
understanding.

A child's silence suggests
intelligence.

FOSTER PARENTS ARE

★

Understanding

Loving

Believing

Inspiring

Aspiring

Uplifting

Consistent

Protective

Thoughtful

Dependable

GRANDPARENTS (rearing
grandchildren) ARE

★

Super - Grand

Super - Patient

Super - Persevering

Super - Wise

Super - Forgiving

Super - Loving

Super - Problem Solving

Super - Exuberant

Super - Exceptional

Super - Generous

Super - !Blessed!

FOREVER PARENTS ARE

★

Caring

Sharing

Exceptional

Thoughtful

Maintaining

Attaining

Mentoring

Astounding

Encouraging

Complimenting

Implementing

MENTORS ARE

★

Unselfish

Believing

Inspiring

Overwhelming

Relentless

Futuristic

Un-abrasive

Unifying

Protective

Constraining

Exemplifying

Containing

TABLE OF CONTENTS

PART ONE

Hope Springs Eternal !!

TABLE OF CONTENTS

PART TWO

Caring, Caring, Caring

Looking for Someone to Care

PART ONE

Hope Springs Eternal !!

TaHeem

A child's smile can warm the heart beyond measure.

TaHeem ~ Age 10

That hot, muggy July day was so very uncomfortable. The window air conditioner was okay, but it was not helping me to cope with the anxiety and tension of my first foster child. My desire to become a foster parent was coming to realization. My deceased husband said to me, "Are you crazy? You must be crazy. These children are messed up." I thought to myself, right now he must be spinning in his grave.

The agency's caseworker called and said, "We are on our way." About fifteen minutes later the doorbell rang. It was the caseworker and TaHeem.

Oh, my. He looked so small, and undernourished. I would later discover it was due to genetics. His mother was a very slightly built woman. The caseworker said to him, "TaHeem, this is your new home. Mrs.

Ruth will be taking care of you." Prior to TaHeem' s coming to my home, the caseworker visited six to eight times during my training, which lasted over three to four months. The caseworker said, "I am leaving now. Mrs. Thacker, call me if you need anything. You have all the phone numbers on the refrigerator. Now you and TaHeem can get acquainted."

TaHeem had given me a big hug when he first came in; but now it seemed as though he was sizing me up. "Do you have children?" he asked. "Yes. I have a daughter and a son, and two grandchildren. The grandchildren are ten and fourteen years old," I replied. "Where are they now?" "My grandchildren are at the school engaging in a summer program for the School of Performing Arts."

Following our conversation TaHeem went into the kitchen. "Are you hungry, TaHeem?" "Yes, I am. Do you have eggs? I love scrambled eggs," he replied. TaHeem ate three scrambled eggs, no toast, just eggs. TaHeem was in his honeymoon mode, and everything was smooth sailing.

The caseworker called the next day. "How is he?" she asked. "Good. He met my grandsons yesterday, and I think he likes them." The caseworker said, "I have some bad news Mrs. Thacker. TaHeem' s mother has been arrested; she was already on probation, and that means she probably will be incarcerated. I am going to have to tell him. He was due to visit her this Saturday. What time will you be home, Mrs. Ruth?"

"I was going to take TaHeem to the playground, should I go ahead with it?" "Yes," the caseworker said "but there is going to be a negative reaction when he finds out. It will be a negative delayed reaction or an immediate negative or both." "Oh, my," I thought to myself, "a problem so soon."

We went to the playground, for about an hour. TaHeem really enjoyed himself. After we arrived back at the house, TaHeem wanted his favorite food – eggs. After eating his eggs (about three hours before dinner), a bag of chips and a candy bar, he seemed pretty content.

The caseworker arrived about two hours later. "TaHeem, I need to talk to you. Come over here and sit with me on the sofa," she said. "You will not be visiting your mother this week. She has been arrested and has been locked up." TaHeem's eyes got really big. His little body fell to the floor. He laid there, face down. He started to cry, sobbing as if he would never stop.

My first instinct was to comfort him, but the anger took over. He said, "Don't touch me!" I looked at the caseworker and asked, "What can I do?" She said, "Let him cry it out." TaHeem's sobbing would start and stop.

About three minutes later, he stopped crying and started staring into space. My youngest grandson (the ten-year-old), suggested that we let him take TaHeem to the restaurant. We both agreed that it sounded like a good idea. TaHeem thought is was a good idea also.

That evening it appeared that everything was okay. TaHeem went into his room to watch TV. The caseworker had advised me to watch him closely. I was on his heels. As soon as TaHeem got into his room he started throwing a temper tantrum. He ran to the window; "I am going to jump out!" he said. Yes, that was one time I was glad that he was skinny and little. I blocked him and held him with all the strength that I could muster. Yes, the caseworker had warned me.

TaHeem started to cry again and I really felt so very helpless. TaHeem," I said, "If you stop crying you can get some of your favorite game cards tomorrow." His favorite game cards were Pac-man. TaHeem stopped crying.

The window episode had to be reported to the agency and the caseworker. The caseworker wanted to know, "Do you want to continue with TaHeem?" "Yes, I do." I answered. "Thank you so much," she replied.

At school TaHeem was put into a special education class (most foster children are Special Education students.) He had an excellent teacher, and this grade school is one of the best in the city, and of course Special Education Was her Specialty.

TaHeem's teacher stayed in constant communication with me, because he was always doing something mischievous. One day he was trying to get out of the car window while the car was moving. I stopped the car. He got out and laid under a tree, with both arms folded on his chest as if he was laying in a casket. When I started up the car, he jumped up and got back in. TaHeem would do quite several things to test my patience, but it was of no consequence.

After seven months, TaHeem's mother was released from prison. She enrolled in a series of parenting programs and it was decided by the courts and D.H.S. that she could be a parent. TaHeem was returned to his mother.

TaHeem was with me for one school year. When he left, I was crying. He looked at me and said; "Mrs. Ruth, why are you crying?" "Because I am going to miss you, TaHeem." He put a wide smile on his face, gave me a big hug and kept waving as he got in the car with the caseworker.

Hope Springs Eternal !!

Drew

A child's resilience transcends understanding.

Drew ~ Age 9

Drew was intelligent, somewhat true to his name. He had a responsive demeanor and was always aware of what was going on around him.

How did this child get into foster care? To this day it is still a puzzle to me. This child clearly came from an upper-middle class family. At the age of nine he could read and tell meanings of words that an eleventh and twelfth grader should know. Drew would grab a book, and say "Mrs. Ruth would you read to me?" Drew would do the reading, not missing one word. I would challenge Drew with four or five syllable words. He knew them!

Drew was lovable, and he liked to be hugged. He also wanted people to love him. That is where his problem came in. Drew was not in my home for a long period of time, but I sensed that his situation could have been molestation. He did not want any of the other boys to come near his bed. Drew wanted to always be in my presence.

As parents and grandparents, and adults, we must start being vigilant in watching behavior in our children that is different or not normal. We do this so that the harm will be stopped and the victim and the violator can get the help they need.

Because of his likeable personality and his smarts, other children were envious of him. There were two other boys in my home when Drew came. They were two and four grades ahead of him, but Drew helped them with their homework.

The caseworker reminded me that he would only be in my home for a short period of time and so he would remain in the school he was already attending. Drew was picked up and returned to my home after school each day. "Mrs. Ruth," Drew would say, "Why don't the boys like me?" "Oh, Drew," I would say, "They like you, but they are not used to a little boy like you being so smart." I was not totally informed about Drew's situation and I agree it was not necessary for me to be informed. But I am assured that wherever he is now, he is at the top of his game. Good success Drew.

Hope Springs Eternal !!

Terry

*A child's hope
can illuminate
the Promise of God.*

Terry ~ Age 10

Terry was a handsome child with a Christian background. His grandmother, who is deceased, was a well-known woman and pastor. Terry 's insecurities were many. His addicted mother would leave him on the corner while she would go get her drugs. "Mrs. Ruth," he confessed to me, "I was so afraid. Sometimes, I would just have to find my way back home." Then he would quote a scripture and say, "I knew that God was still in control."

Terry's knowledge of the Bible was so very awesome. He said that God was going to forgive his mother and that God was going to get her back to him. Terry had walked away from his former foster parent and the police had to find him. He had an extremely bad temper that prevented him from positive interaction with other children. School was the ultimate challenge for him. Every day there would be an incident of some type. Yet, through all of this, his intelligence shined through.

One day he decided that absolutely not... he was not going to school. Mr. Huff, his favorite teacher, who also had been a foster child, called me. "Mrs. Ruth, where is Terry. I did not see him for roll-call." "Mr. Huff," I said, "Terry told me that he was not going to school today." Mr. Huff replied, "I am on break. Do you mind if I come over and get him?" I said, "Mr. Huff. I would love it."

Mr. Huff came over: "Where is he, Mrs. Ruth?" "He is upstairs hiding under the bunk bed," I answered. He went up the steps, and laying face down on the floor, reached under the bunk bed and pulled Terry out. Mr. Huff and Terry walked arm in arm out the door to the car, and Mr. Huff drove off with Terry to school. Well now we do have dedicated teachers in these school districts.

Terry's intelligence was apparent to Mr. Huff also. At the report card meeting Mr. Huff showed me a project that Terry had put together. He stated, "Mrs. Ruth you are not going to believe what I am going to show you. This project that Terry did is amazing. It was about birds. It was so thorough and informative that you would not believe that a troubled child could have done it. Terry's grade was an A-minus; I thought it was worth an A-plus."

Terry continued to improve. He stopped asking me if he could sit on my lap. He also started interacting with the other two children, and he would smile more often.

Every now and then he Terry would ask me, "Mrs. Ruth, why did my grandmother have to die?" "Terry, we all have to die sooner or later," I answered. Your grandmother left quite a legacy, and you, Mr. Terry, are a part of that legacy. Your grandmother would be very proud of you." He smiled so generously and came over and gave me a big hug.

Terry had only one more incident before leaving my home. I dropped him off to school and almost as soon as I returned home there was a phone call from the school. Terry found out about that Mr. Huff was not in the classroom because he had a very bad cold. Mrs. Ruth, the principal said, "You will have to come and get Terry. He has fallen on the floor and we are trying to restrain him." When I arrived back at the school, the principal and the substitute teacher were both trying to console Terry. He saw me and he stopped crying and said, "Mrs. Ruth, take me home. Mr. Huff is not here."

Soon, after this, there was a meeting with D.H.S. and the agency. This was to decide whether Terry would be living with an Aunt, who had been clean, and Terry told me that he did like her. In fact, she had visited him while he was in my care. I recently saw her at a church function. She told me that Terry had graduated from college and was working toward his master's degree... Onward and Upward Terry.

Hope Springs Eternal !!

DeLando

*A child's concept
can put an adult
on notice.*

DeLando ~ Age 12

DeLando was of Latin and Afro-American heritage. He was the most handsome, dapper kid that had been placed on this planet called Earth.

DeLando's mother had engaged in prostitution, to fund a drug addiction. DeLando would say and make statements that came directly from the streets. He would yell to women from my car window, "Walk it baby, you're looking good, and you're humped back there." DeLando you cannot yell at women from my car window," I said to him. "Mrs. Ruth, I like girls with big butts." "DeLando, I am not interested in the kind of girls you like. You really need to concentrate on getting an education," I said to him.

DeLando would look at himself in the mirror and talk to himself: "Hi there you handsome guy, you're really good looking," he would say. He would make fun of the other children, calling them homey or ugly. DeLando was also a huge liar; he could lie about everything, even when it was not necessary to lie.

DeLando liked basketball. "Mrs. Ruth. You have to come see me play," he said. "My coach at school says I'm good. I think that I am the best on the team." Of course, DeLando would say that. I went to see him play basketball. What a show-off! DeLando made the nets from center court; DeLando was picking up the rebounds; DeLando was chasing the ball off the court. DeLando played some basketball that day. When the game was over, the coach saw him with me. "Who is she," the coach asked. "This is my godmother," DeLando said to the coach. "She needs to come to the games when we are playing a really good team," replied the coach. DeLando was grinning from ear to ear.

When we got home from the game most of DeLando's time was spent on the phone talking to girls. "DeLando get off of the phone and do your homework." "Mrs. Ruth, give me just five more minutes." I always listened to his conversations. DeLando would say things to the girls that were inferior. He would criticize the way the girls wore their hair, the kind of clothes they wore, and their physical structure. He said to one girl, "Your butt is not big enough." DeLando did not get his five minutes. I hung the phone up.

The Principal of the school that DeLando was attending called me himself. "Mrs. Ruth," he said; "DeLando had some girl in the hall and was trying to convince her to go into the boy's restroom and have sex with him." This incident had to be reported to the agency. The caseworker increased his therapeutic sessions and assigned him to a different therapist. DeLando denied everything and went on a mission to seduce the therapist by telling her that she was pretty and sharp and good-looking! The therapist was extremely unimpressed. She told him that he was a child, and that he needed a "timeout!"

DeLando was not only vain, but crafty and cunning. He said to the therapist, "I am going to report you to DHS." She said to him, "I AM DHS!" DeLando was angry; he walked out of the therapist's office.

I went looking for him in the hall. He was on the phone. "Who are you talking to DeLando?" I asked. "My uncle," he replied. "Mrs. Ruth, I don't want to live with you anymore." "Okay, DeLando. I will call the agency tomorrow. Maybe, they can arrange for you to live with your uncle," I responded.

I called the agency the next day and they told me that they had been trying to have DeLando's uncle be his foster parent. Wow! This was the first time DeLando was truthful!

I breathed a sigh of relief – yes, this narcissistic lover child was getting to be a challenge.

DeLando had seen an athletic sleeve at one of the sports stores, and made no bones about it; he wanted that sports sleeve. "Mrs. Ruth," he said, "If you buy me that sleeve, I will suck your toes." I did not know what he was talking about. Of course, I called the agency because knowing DeLando, it probably would have a sexual connotation.

When I called the agency I was connected to the director. I disclosed to her what DeLando had said. She said. "Excuse me, hold on. I will be right back." She either went to research the statement or to laugh. When she came back to the phone, she said, "Mrs. Ruth, can you put up with him for about two more weeks? We believe his uncle is going to take him." The uncle called me, and we talked about DeLando and his demeanor. He thanked me for putting up with him.

In about fourteen days, five hours and thirty minutes the caseworker came to pick up Mr. DeLando; who decided he wanted a kiss on the cheek before he left. "Mrs. Ruth," he said, "You are a good-looking old woman." "Thank you, DeLando" I said. "Try to behave yourself."

I did not believe in a child not having any contact with their parents, but in this case, I thought about finding out if I had that option.

Hope Springs Eternal !!

A CHILD IS AMAZING

★

A child's laughter can make
an angel sing.

A child's innocence creates an
aura of wisdom.

A child's smile can warm the
heart beyond measure.

A child's hands are the
potential artists of the world.

A child's hope can illuminate
the Promise of God.

A child's strength can move
the highest mountain.

A child's love can create the
most beautiful universe.

A child's concept can put an adult on notice.

A child's peace can be found in a sea of turmoil.

A child's understanding can be the anchor for a large ship.

A child's talents and gifts show they are given by God.

A child's tolerance can be magical.

A child's wisdom is an unbelievable protection.

A child's resilience transcends understanding.

A child's silence suggests intelligence.

FOSTER PARENTS ARE

★

Understanding

Loving

Believing

Inspiring

Aspiring

Uplifting

Consistent

Protective

Thoughtful

Dependable

GRANDPARENTS (rearing grandchildren) ARE

★

Super - Grand

Super - Patient

Super - Persevering

Super - Wise

Super - Forgiving

Super - Loving

Super - Problem Solving

Super - Exuberant

Super - Exceptional

Super - Generous

Super - !Blessed!

FOREVER PARENTS ARE

★

Caring

Sharing

Exceptional

Thoughtful

Maintaining

Attaining

Mentoring

Astounding

Encouraging

Complimenting

Implementing

MENTORS ARE

★

Unselfish

Believing

Inspiring

Overwhelming

Relentless

Futuristic

Un-abrasive

Unifying

Protective

Constraining

Exemplifying

Containing

Steve

*A child's wisdom
is an
unbelievable protection.*

Steve ~ Age 13

All the children were coming and going. During that period of time, I had become a parental legal guardian to two of the youth. Steve was one of them. His mother has given birth to eleven children while still testing positive for drug abuse. All the children were in the foster care system.

His father went to parenting classes and was trying to play a positive role in his life, but the changing of girlfriends every three to four months was not a good thing. "Do not introduce Steve to all of these different women," I said to his father, "unless you are serious about her and going to be married." Well now, that was water running off a duck's back. "Mrs. Ruth, you are so old fashioned," his father commented and burst out laughing.

Steve would come back after a visit with his father and he was anxious to know if I had seen his girlfriend, who lived on the block. "Why do you want to see Angie, Steve?" I asked him. "I have something to tell her, Mrs. Ruth;" he replied. "Steve, have you read the book that was part of your school assignment?" I asked. "I read some of it, but I have two more weeks before I have to turn my report in."

After one of the visits with his father, Steve took Angie to the fast-food restaurant's restroom. The security guard found them. He told me about the incident when I went in to get some fries. "Ms. Ruth, Steve was in the rest-room moving and grooving with his girlfriend," he said. "I gave them a good warning." "Alright, then." I thanked the security guard and said to him, "Let me see how he does without his cell phone and television."

Steve had a passion for hanging out with the wrong people, "Steve do you realize that you are defined by the kind of crowd you hang around with?" I said to him. "Mrs. Ruth, my friends are okay. Lots of them are foster children like me," he said. "I heard Jamal cussing the f-word in everything he said, and he cannot do that in my house." Steve shrugged his shoulder. "All right, Mrs. Ruth," he said.

About eleven-thirty, one Saturday night, I smelled this not -so-pleasant odor coming from my basement. As I went down the basement steps the smell became more commanding and powerful. As I got closer to the bottom step I heard the sound of feet rushing out of the basement door. Yes, you guessed it! The boys were smoking marijuana to get high. Steve was due to get his cell phone and television back; of course, that did not happen.

Steve ran track in school. "How can you run track and smoke pot?" I asked. "Oh, I don't smoke pot all the time, Mrs. Ruth, only when I am feeling depressed." "Steve, why are you feeling depressed?" I asked. "My teacher told me my grades might not be good enough to go to that military school that I want to go to." "Steve, I have been telling you to go to tutoring for any subject that you are having a problem with. You can always improve with tutoring." Steve went to four tutoring classes and stopped.

Steve's depression was not just from girls. His grandmother had throat cancer. Steve and his grandmother had a very close relationship. I would take him to see her at her senior citizen apartment. He wanted to go see her when she was in and out of the hospital. I tried to discourage too many visits to the hospital, because I noticed the depression.

Steve's grandmother finally passed. By this time Steve was fifteen years of age. He had made it to the Military School. Steve was still liking Angie, and I was hoping she would be a good influence, but sometimes she was like putty and clay in his hands.

Steve was still running track and was awarded a trophy for a winning run. He attended college and he did well the first two years; and then he wanted the challenge of going into the Military. He is the father of two children.

Hope Springs Eternal !!

Drey & Kelko

*A child's peace
can be found
in a sea of turmoil.*

Drey ~ 10 and Kelko ~ 7

Drey and Kelko are brothers who were placed in foster care because their mother became mentally incompetent due to dependency on painkillers (that were discontinued) and crack-cocaine. The agency stated she is in recovery but in a very fragile state. The family was from out-of-state and this caused the children to be placed.

Drey was muscular and kind of tall. Kelko was the direct opposite, short and stocky, but a good-looking little boy. Drey did not appreciate Kelko's good looks. He resented him in all his actions. If Kelko was trying to sit down, Drey would move the chair so that Kelko could fall to the floor. Drey would push Kelko down the stairs and trip him with his foot. My work was cut out for me, with Drey having this kind of attitude toward his brother.

The caseworker called me: "Mrs. Ruth, do you think you can take the boys to therapy?" "I most certainly can," I responded. "They really need to go to the therapist. Drey has a problem concerning his brother." "What has been going on?" she asked. I told her what had been occurring and she gave me a date and time to take them.

Meanwhile, I had to keep a good eye on Drey. "Mrs. Ruth, Drey does not like me," said Kelko. I replied, "You just let me know when he is bullying you around and he will get that new game taken away that I brought for him." Kelko was a very agreeable child, and he always wanted Drey to like him.

On the day of the boys' appointment Drey was lying on the sofa and Kelko was sitting on the edge of the sofa. Drey raised his foot so high and hard he put his feet right into Kelko's eyes. I heard a scream and ran to see what was going on. Kelko was crying and trying to tell me what had happened between sobs. Drey lied and said he had done nothing! I went to the fridge to get ice for Kelko's eye. "Oh. My!" I said to myself. I wonder if the boys should be placed separately.

Upon arriving at the therapist's office Kelko's eye swelling had gone down, but you could tell that he had been hit. The therapist talked to me first. I relayed to her all of my thoughts concerning the boys. "Maybe we do need to separate them, Mrs. Ruth. But you know we like to keep family together. This is kind of serious with Drey. He might be envious of Kelko's good looks and he probably needs a lengthy period of help," she said. "When you see his eye," I commented, "you will see what I am talking about."

The next person the therapist talked to was Drey. He was with her a long time. After Drey finished talking to the therapist she said to me, "Mrs. Ruth, I know that you have to get Kelko to the doctor to have his eye examined, but I will call you this evening to give you our decision on separating the boys."

We left the therapist's office, hurrying because Kelko's appointment was in the next half hour. We arrived, and the doctor examined his eye. He told me to continue with the ice on it and that it would be okay.

On the way home, when we had gotten on my street, I saw this man with a pit-bull dog. He said to me. "Are you Dray's mother? I want him to come over to my house and walk Sampson." "Drey," I said, "have you been walking this dog?" "Yes, Mrs. Ruth," Drey said. "Drey, I did not give you permission. Pit-bull dogs are very dangerous, and you do not have my permission to walk this dog."

The man, hearing our conversation, started to walk away. I said to him. "Do not let Drey walk your dog. He does not have my permission." "Oh, no," said the man, "I thought you knew." "No. I did not know about it. You as an adult should have asked me if he could do it." The man, whose name I did not know but I had seen him in various stores in the neighborhood, had the reputation of being a drug dealer. "Okay maam, I won't let him walk this dog anymore," he said, and he walked away.

Drey appeared to be angry. I said to him "Drey, you are a child and you must learn to obey and listen to me."

The therapist called me in the early evening. She relayed to me that she would recommend that the boys be separated and that Drey would be having ongoing therapy sessions. This information from the therapist made me feel a whole lot better about the brothers' problems.

Drey and Kelko were placed in two different homes about a month later.

★

Hope Springs Eternal !!

Elijah

*A child's talents and gifts
show that they are
given by God.*

Elijah ~ 11

Elijah was being reared by his grandmother. His mom had left home about one year after she had given birth to him. Elijah's mom was nowhere to be found and because of the stress involved, his grandmother got sick. She was diagnosed with stage four breast cancer. His grandmother could no longer care for him.

Elijah's personality was very cautious. Elijah, most times would stare at a person before he would say 'hello.' Or 'Hi" to them. He was quiet and reserved; and he was always waiting for the other person to break the ice. When the caseworker brought him to the house, he did not say one word. He looked at me. While the caseworker was talking to me, he was continually staring at me, and not uttering a word. Finally, and it seemed like an eternity, Elijah said, "Do you have any potato chips?" "Yes, I do. Elijah," I responded. It was a small bag of chips, and it seemed as though he ate them so fast that he had inhaled them.

The caseworker was preparing to leave. "Elijah loves potato chips and kit-kat bars. Mrs. Ruth, you can use those two treats as rewards for him." "Oh, Ms. Kelly," I said to her, "Thank you for the heads-up suggestion, but is he always this quiet?" "Oh, no," she said, "when he plays games and watches TV he becomes a part of what is going on." This I had to see, and so I found the Xbox, and sure enough, he was talking to the characters in the game and making all kinds of noise.

Elijah was shy with real people. I found out later that he had been molested by the grandmother's boyfriend.

Elijah loved to go to church and that was kind of unusual for a child his age. He would say to me, "Ms. Ruth, God loves me, and everything is going to be alright." The other children liked Elijah because he never would make waves or be a trouble maker. He would just follow along with what they were doing. No, Elijah was not a leader, and that turned out to be a problem.

The boys at school decided they were bored at study period, so bored that on of them had a match, lit it and set the waste basket on fire in the classroom. Because it was the students that Elijah would be with, he was implicated in the situation. "Ms. Ruth, I did not do it;" Elijah said, "and it happened so fast that I did not see who did it." "Elijah, the principal told me that it was the boys you hang out with at school," I said to him, "and you are going to be suspended right along with them. Elijah remember, I told you to choose your friends very carefully." Elijah and his friends were suspended for four days. I felt badly for him knowing that with his being shy, he would just go along with the crowd. But he soon came to learn that you are defined by the company you keep. "Ms. Ruth, I want to go to a different school," he said. "I responded, "Elijah, it is not the school that is the problem."

I related the incident to the mentor at the church what had occurred. Deacon Anderson suggested that the church had started a youth program for boys-to-fifteen with all kinds of activities that taught how to be on good behavior, and how to refrain from being friends with troublemakers. This was a very good thing for Elijah, because he really did like church and church activities.

Elijah is an Assistant Pastor at a church in the city and he is doing well and thriving. He has become engaged to a wonderful young lady.

Hope Springs Eternal !!

Reese

A child's love
can create
the most beautiful universe.

Reese ~ 15

Reese was an intricate part of the children in my life, but he did not come from an agency. He simply walked across the street when he was coming home from school at the tender age of six and announced to me and his grandmother, "Ms. Ruth is my godmother." His grandmother and I looked at each other and we laughed. "What did you say, Reese?" his grandmother asked him. He repeated "I said Ms. Ruth is my godmother." "Okay, Reese. I am your godmother." From that day on Reese was in and out of my house almost as if he be lived there.

Reese was being reared by his grandmother because his mother had mental issues and she was also a user of drugs. His grandmother had been granted legal custody. Reese was alert with a high intelligence of the streets, He not only lived with his grandmother, he lived with her three sons who were known as drug users and drug pushers in the area. My ambition was to let him know that he could become anything he wanted to be, and rise above this environment.

Every positive activity with children that I was involved in within my church, I made sure Reese attended. When he became nine years old, he was baptized. Reese had a hunger and thirst to learn about God.

The environment at his grandmother's house was starting to give him negative habits. Reese started to steal from church members. The members would come to me, and I would find items and money right then and there in his pockets. I talked to his grandmother and she called the agency that oversaw Reese. He was placed into scheduled therapy. After he finished therapy, he was a great deal better.

By the age of fifteen his grandmother had passed, and he came to live with me. "See, Ms. Ruth," he said, "I knew what I was doing when I said you were my godmother."

Reese was not attending school on a regular basis and it was the one thing that I had to address. I had to provide an initiative and rewards. Reese, being a teenager, loved monetary rewards. An allowance was set up for attending school every day. His teachers wanted to know what had happened. Why was he attending school on a regular basis? I talked to them and they were extremely happy about the improvement.

Reese graduated from High School and is attending a Community College. While he is really trying to do something with his life, there is excess of smoking weed. I talk to him often. Reese promised me he would stop that excessive practice, as he has met a very nice young woman who encourages and inspires him to be the best he can be.

★

Hope Springs Eternal !!

A CHILD IS AMAZING
★

A child's laughter can make
an angel sing.

A child's innocence creates an
aura of wisdom.

A child's smile can warm the
heart beyond measure.

A child's hands are the
potential artists of the world.

A child's hope can illuminate
the Promise of God.

A child's strength can move
the highest mountain.

A child's love can create the
most beautiful universe.

A child's concept can put an adult on notice.

A child's peace can be found in a sea of turmoil.

A child's understanding can be the anchor for a large ship.

A child's talents and gifts show they are given by God.

A child's tolerance can be magical.

A child's wisdom is an unbelievable protection.

A child's resilience transcends understanding.

A child's silence suggests intelligence.

FOSTER PARENTS ARE

★

Understanding

Loving

Believing

Inspiring

Aspiring

Uplifting

Consistent

Protective

Thoughtful

Dependable

GRANDPARENTS (rearing
grandchildren) ARE

★

Super - Grand

Super - Patient

Super - Persevering

Super - Wise

Super - Forgiving

Super - Loving

Super - Problem Solving

Super - Exuberant

Super - Exceptional

Super - Generous

Super - !Blessed!

FOREVER PARENTS ARE

★

Caring

Sharing

Exceptional

Thoughtful

Maintaining

Attaining

Mentoring

Astounding

Encouraging

Complimenting

Implementing

MENTORS ARE

★

Unselfish

Believing

Inspiring

Overwhelming

Relentless

Futuristic

Un-abrasive

Unifying

Protective

Constraining

Exemplifying

Containing

Larry

A child's understanding
can be the anchor
for a large ship.

Larry ~ 13

Larry was the child who would always ask questions about everything. Larry was put into foster care after a series of challenging circumstances. Right away you could tell he had been pretty well cared for. His mom was a registered nurse who became addicted to drugs because of a failed marriage and the negative occurrences. His grandmother began caring for him and she was killed in an automobile accident.

Larry wanted to know, "Ms. Ruth why did all these things happen?" "Larry, I do not know. But one thing I do know is- that you are a smart, intelligent, young man and you can be anything you want to be. Even a rocket scientist." "Ms. Ruth, you make me feel so good." "Larry, I mean every word I am saying to you. Your teacher told me that if you calm down and learn to take instructions you could be at the head of the class," I said.

Larry's teacher reported that he was out of order in class. In a couple of weeks the agency provided a person to sit with him in class (Wraparound Program). Mr. Watson, the wraparound person, always kept me informed of Larry's progress and of course he kept the agency aware.

Larry was almost fourteen years old and experiencing puberty, and the girls were starting to be a distraction. "Ms. Ruth, do you think I am too young to have a girlfriend?" "Yes, you are to young, Larry; your education is first." "Mr. Watson told me the same thing, but I get a funny feeling when I look at Andrea. I get excited!" I had to go into the next room, because I was smiling, and I almost laughed. I did not want Larry to see me doing that!

Larry was participating in class and concentrating on his classwork, so the wraparound person, Mr. Watson, was not needed anymore. The report cards were getting better and better and Larry was on his way. He wanted to go to the military high school and the grades were good enough for him to get in.

Larry liked football very much and he said to me, "Ms. Ruth, I am going to try out for the team. I will have to practice over the summer, but I don't care. I think I can make it." "I think you can make it too, Larry," I said. He was a fast runner and I immediately thought running back, but they made him a wide receiver and running back. Larry became a very good football player and his interests turned toward being the very best on the team. Larry had a competitive spirit and that was a very good thing.

A distant cousin showed up and she was trained and cleared by the agency for Larry's kinship foster parent.

★

Hope Springs Eternal !!

Ellio

★

*A child's laughter
can make
an angel sing.*

Ellio ~ 10

Ellio was of Native American descent and a mixture of Black, Indian and Caucasian heritage. He was born to make people laugh. Ellio's jokes were somewhat corny, but his presentation was so sincere; in that alone they would make you laugh. "Ms. Ruth, why did the chicken cross the road?" Just to get a laugh, Ellio would move the chair if one of the other children was getting ready to sit down.

Ellio's mom had abandoned him. His dad was trying to take care of him and had done a criminal act and was incarcerated. Ellio had quite a few problems, and I do believe that the comedian in him was a way of forgetting about himself and making other people laugh.

Ellio was in a play at school and he was playing the role of the class clown. The only problem was that the class clown was always getting into trouble. As soon as the teacher would exit the classroom, the class clown would spring into action making all the kids laugh. "Ellio," I said, "do not take this play too seriously, because if you do, you will always stay in trouble." "Okay, Ms. Ruth. I will be okay."

Ellio played the role very well, and he received quite a few compliments. Mr. Jay; his teacher had already told me that he thought Ellio would probably be an actor when he grows up. Ellio was blushing all over the place when the play was over.

"Ms. Ruth, are you taking me out to dinner? You told me that if I do well in the play, that you would take me out." "Yes, Ellio." I responded, "Where would you like to go?" "I want to go to the Buffet Dinner Restaurant and eat until my belly can't hold any more." "Okay, Ellio, that's where we will go, but I do not want you to eat yourself sick." We went to the buffet; Ellio and his friend Kato. I think Kato was trying to eat himself sick, too.

When Ellio went for his once a month therapy session, his therapist and I agreed that he was making positive progress. The caseworker visited the next week. She stated that Ellio's father was to be released from prison and that he might be given a chance for parenting. I had my concerns about that and I shared them with the caseworker.

Ellio had been showing his underwear at school, and the therapist had told me that it could be a sign that he might have been molested. My concern was that the father might have been involved with this. The caseworker agreed that since the father was coming out of prison, he probably should not be given custody of Ellio. The father was not given custody.

A relative who was a minister was cleared by the agency; and Mr. Ellio had a loving home to go to and thrive in. That was my prayer for him. He is doing well today; Ellio is a minister, also.

Hope Springs Eternal !!

Miguel

*A child's strength
can move
the highest mountain.*

Miguel ~ 11

Miquel was very inquisitive; always asking questions about almost everything. (Most foster children are inquisitive.) Miguel's most frequent question was "When is my mom coming back to get me?" Miquel was eleven years old, very energetic and intelligent. He was happy to be Latino and when he became angry, he would curse the other children in Spanish. "Ms. Ruth," Miquel said to me, "Do you know any Spanish:" "Only the curse words Miquel," I replied.

Miquel was a very good-looking boy and even though he was only eleven the teenage girls was giving him the eye. "Ms. Ruth," Miquel said "Shana tried to kiss me, right in front of the house today." "You tell Shana I want to talk to her," I said to Miquel. I really had to watch the girls with Miquel. "Are girls and women supposed to get hit when they get bad or get on your nerves?" Miquel asked. I responded, "No Miquel. That is not correct to hit girls or women. You can further discuss it with Ms. Jean, your therapist. You have an appointment next Wednesday." "My mom's boyfriend hit her all the time," Miquel said, "and all she would do is cry. She never hit him back. I think that is why she would get high, so she could just forget about it," Miquel said. "When I get older, I am going to hurt somebody if they mess with my mother." "Miquel," I said, "You are such a handsome and smart boy; get an education and you will be able to help yourself and your mother." Miquel said, "Ms. Ruth, when is my mother coming out of the rehab?" "We will know when your caseworker, Ms. Scurry comes to see you in a couple of weeks."

Miquel wanted to go to summer camp, but the application for camp had to be in three weeks before entering. Miquel was very anxious about seeing his mother, but after rehab she had to serve one year for shoplifting. Knowing this would really be a serious negative for Miquel, and this negative did become a disappointing reality.

Miquel had to be enrolled in school, because Summer had turned into Fall. His feelings about his mother's delayed return played out in class. Although his IQ was very good, the disappointment affected his performance and behavior in school. Miquel's caseworker and I discussed some kind of compensation. We came up with the idea to enroll him in Karate classes. Miquel's demeanor and outlook slowly started to change. He became more confident in himself; grades at school improved and he was on his way to earning his first karate belt.

His mom had to serve only one half of her sentence. She attended parenting classes and Miquel was reunited with his mom by the end of the school year.

Hope Springs Eternal !!

Devon

A child's hands
are the potential artists
of the world.

Devon ~ Age 14

Devon was one of the oldest children that I had fostered. He was very independent but had an extremely selfish and cold demeanor. His attitude toward everything was negative; he trusted no one, and he was always saying things like, "He is a phony." "Ms. Ruth," he replied to me, "Why are people lying all the time?" I responded by saying to him, "Devon it is the kind of people that you are with and take in to trust as a friend."

The caseworker told me that Devon had been handed off after his mother passed, from relative to relative, and he had become a disciplinary problem. This is how he finally ended up in foster care. I thought to myself; the therapist's work is really going to be difficult with this young man.

He had just started the school year, and I had to go to the school for two situations that had occurred. I talked to his homeroom teacher, "Mr. James, can you give him some type of special classroom project?" "Yes, Ms. Ruth, I will come up with something for Devon to do." Mr. James was very helpful. Devon was responsible for collecting books and keeping chalk and erasers intact for the blackboard, and quite a few other things that needed to be done.

I heard of a mentoring program that was affiliated with PAL (the Police Athletic League), and Devon was enrolled into the program. I thought it was all boys but somehow or other Devon had met a young lady and he wanted me to meet her. "Ms. Ruth," Devon said, "She is real." "Devon you are too young to be able to determine the reality of a relationship," I said to him. "Ms. Ruth, I will be fifteen in two weeks. I want to have a birthday party and you can meet Taneesa; because I'm in love." Devon, how many times do you want me to tell you that you are too young for that," I said.

Two weeks went by and I let Devon have the party… in the basement. I had to go down there a few times, first the music was too loud; and then things got too quiet; and after that, someone tried to smoke weed.

Yes, and Taneesa was nice, but she appeared to be older than Devon. "Ms. Ruth, it is nice to meet you," she said; "and I am going to keep Devon out of trouble and cool." "Don't keep him too cool," I said to her; "But if you are good in math you could help him. His math is not good, and he won't get up in the morning and go to tutoring." "I will help him, Ms. Ruth." "Taneesa, the tutoring will have to be done in the dining room at the table. It cannot be done in private." "Oh, that's okay," she said, "I know he has to concentrate on the work." I think I like her (talking to myself again).

The math tutoring started the next week. They were in the dining room watching TV. I got up, went to the bathroom, and on my way back downstairs, Devon had gotten up, gone over to Taneesa and had her sitting on his lap. Well that was the end of that tutoring session.

Devon, if I give you extra money in your allowance would you make a sincere effort to get up in the morning for math tutoring?" "Yes, I will," Ms. Ruth, "but it will have to be five dollars." "Oh, no, not five dollars but three dollars, and we will see how it goes. You can get up to five, you already have eight dollars a week and three makes it eleven." We made the agreement.

Devon started getting up and soon it became a routine. His grades got better and better. Devon was getting more confident. He started running track, and did very well at that. He won a track meet at school, trophy and all. The caseworker also was able to limit his therapy sessions to one per month instead of two.

It was kind of troubling when the caseworker told me that yet another relative had been cleared for Devon to live with. Of, course there was not anything that I could do about that.

Hope Springs Eternal !!

A CHILD IS AMAZING

★

A child's laughter can make
an angel sing.

A child's innocence creates an
aura of wisdom.

A child's smile can warm the
heart beyond measure.

A child's hands are the
potential artists of the world.

A child's hope can illuminate
the Promise of God.

A child's strength can move
the highest mountain.

A child's love can create the
most beautiful universe.

A child's concept can put an adult on notice.

A child's peace can be found in a sea of turmoil.

A child's understanding can be the anchor for a large ship.

A child's talents and gifts show they are given by God.

A child's tolerance can be magical.

A child's wisdom is an unbelievable protection.

A child's resilience transcends understanding.

A child's silence suggests intelligence.

FOSTER PARENTS ARE

★

Understanding

Loving

Believing

Inspiring

Aspiring

Uplifting

Consistent

Protective

Thoughtful

Dependable

GRANDPARENTS (rearing grandchildren) ARE

★

Super - Grand

Super - Patient

Super - Persevering

Super - Wise

Super - Forgiving

Super - Loving

Super - Problem Solving

Super - Exuberant

Super - Exceptional

Super - Generous

Super - !Blessed!

FOREVER PARENTS ARE

★

Caring

Sharing

Exceptional

Thoughtful

Maintaining

Attaining

Mentoring

Astounding

Encouraging

Complimenting

Implementing

MENTORS ARE

★

Unselfish

Believing

Inspiring

Overwhelming

Relentless

Futuristic

Un-abrasive

Unifying

Protective

Constraining

Exemplifying

Containing

Looking for Someone to Care

PART TWO

Caring, Caring, Caring

TABLE OF CONTENTS

PART TWO

Caring, Caring, Caring

Insight: Foster Parenting and Therapy

FOSTER PARENTS ARE

Understanding

Loving

Believing

Inspiring

Aspiring

Uplifting

Consistent

Protective

Thoughtful

Dependable

Insight:
Foster Parenting and Therapy

Therapy sessions are very helpful with that negative thinking process, but at the end of the day the children still love their parents. This is the reason most all agencies have a reunification program.

Earlier in the book I mentioned a seven-year-old who cried all the way through his homework, learning how to do his homework all by himself. Another child, who needed someone to sit with him in class (Wraparound), become an honor roll student in two years.

Parenting is a challenge all by "itself." One does not need drugs or anything else to make it more difficult. Experiences and teachable moments come to us in many forms, people, places and things. I, as a foster parent had a challenging journey that was enjoyed. Oh, yes. There were moments I wanted to throw the towel in the ring and give up; but one of these beautiful disenfranchised children would make me laugh, by doing something unexplainably positive.

There is a program that most of the Foster Agencies have wherein the Foster Parent becomes the child's legal guardian and the child can stay in the foster home until the age of eighteen years old. This program requires additional training and microscopic viewing by the agency, and finalization by the courts. The end result is that the child feels more like a member of the family. The child is no longer moved from home to home. Yes, yes, yes, it takes a village to raise a child, a city, and a nation.

As you are providing a positive and loving environment for the foster child, you must remember genetics also play a role; whether they be positive or negative. Once again, your tolerance and training show up (smile).

One more very important fact: Remember how you wanted to be treated as a child? You wanted treats, and ice cream – applying these memories will make "you" an excellent Foster Resource-Parent.

I hope you are enjoying the book, and becoming inspired, even to the point of cleaning out that room you are using for a closet or storage room and becoming a challenged person by giving a victimized child the comforts of a loving home.

Caring, Caring, Caring

Parenting Complexities and Genetics

GRANDPARENTS (rearing grandchildren) ARE

★

Super - Grand

Super - Patient

Super - Persevering

Super - Wise

Super - Forgiving

Super - Loving

Super - Problem Solving

Super - Exuberant

Super - Exceptional

Super - Generous

Super - !Blessed!

Parenting Complexities and Genetics

Perplexing and amazing and a mixture of continuing emotions, somewhat describes "Parenting," although there are a multitude of complicated descriptions that can be made to describe this art of *Parenting.* Someone implied that it is like waiting to exhale and while waiting the occurrences and situations become even more complex.

Many parents are working two jobs in our economy, and that alone is a build-up to not enough time to give to children. While trying to improve the environment of the child with a better school, and an improved neighborhood means that money is at the top of the list. The advent of bullying and school-active shooters adds another whole dimension to the *Parenting Process.* This makes parenting even more difficult.

We, all know that getting an education is the most important positivity that we can convey to our children. While, we emphasize this, we must also remind ourselves that one must try to give as much family time that is possible, for the mental security of the family is found in certain skills that a parent acquires.

How do we do this? Trail and error? Grounding? Time-outs? Or do we wait until we need a *Family Therapist.* Oh, well, whoever made the statement that *"Parenting was a walk in the Park?"* was totally incorrect!

We ask ourselves so Many questions, but the answers are not there. As parents, we are dealing also with genetics. Every child of course has developed their own personalities. We are all familiar with this.

How do you handle *Ginger's straight A-report card, versus April's C-report with one D?*

You want to praise Ginger for her achievement, but not in the presence of April. You do not want April to become discouraged or resentful of Ginger. Here, we are again in another parent's situation. Now! Who has the solution to all of this?

What about Marc who runs track has five trophies and is trying out for the football team as a running back; he is extremely confident that he is going to make it.

What is going on with Casey who lays around most of the time and does not want to take the trash out when it is his turn to do it. Casey and Marc share the room together. Marc's side of the room is neat, everything in place. Casey's side of the room is a total mess; yet as parents we must deal with both sides of the spectrum.

Being unaware that Jerome, the adult child who is joined in holy matrimony, is hitting his wife when she disagrees with him, you tell most people when asked, "Oh, Jerome has a beautiful marriage." Jerome's dad would also hit you if you disagreed with him. That is why the two of them are not together. Genetics in this occurrence? Most people would say "YES. Yes. Yes."

One young girl at the age of eleven made a speech at the Old Family Church. On the way back to her seat, she heard two older women say, "Did you hear that?" One said to the other, "Well, you know her granddaddy was a very good speaking and teaching preacher."

Genetics? It seems somewhat evident that genes are passed on. Why does that brown boy have auburn hair? A look at the family tree reveals that his great-grandfather was Irish.

When visiting your doctor, you know that genetics are important by the questions you are asked on your form. As a parent, not only are you dealing with the child you have but the Aunt Marie, Grand-mom Alice and Aunt Gloria all rolled up into one individual.

What about the geniuses of the world who master algebra, trigonometry, calculus, physics at the usual age of ten, eleven or even twelve? A perfect array and arrangement of genes taking habitation in the mind of a child. Yes! Genes, genetics play a powerful role in the mental and physical make-up of children and adults.

★

Caring, Caring, Caring

Role of the Foster Parent

FOREVER PARENTS ARE

★

Caring

Sharing

Exceptional

Thoughtful

Maintaining

Attaining

Mentoring

Astounding

Encouraging

Complimenting

Implementing

Role of the Foster Parent

As in the role of the foster parent, in natural parenting of our own children we must learn to develop an endearing patience, as we try to motivate and mold our youth to be responsible adults. The challenge that present themselves are endless. Very, rarely are the times that we can give grown children advice and they listen. These, adult-children, do not hear our voice, and we must stand and watch *exactly what we tell them not to do, come into fruition.* Referring to teachable moments for parenting, of course it must be during the child's early years. It is, indeed, frustrating to see what you the parent have taught them go up in smoke; yet it is rewarding when finally, you see signs of "I get it." As a parent your mind is saying "it is about time that you get it."

Responding to negative actions from a child or a grown adult-child can be "Oh," so challenging; if the response from the parent comes into play in the same negative manner. Remaining calm is very difficult, but it is key to trying to find a peaceful solution. Committing oneself to foster parenting is complex, as it is somewhat instinctive. The female role is the best displayed in parenting. While the male may abandon the child and the family-it takes huge negatives for the female to abandon her child. This is why we see a situation where a mother has given up a child or children, there is usually a dire unusual set of circumstances involved.

What chance, if any; do we have to see our child project what they have been taught. This is very slim pickings. Yet, there is hope, love, faith, understanding and when there is life, it is never too late or too soon. You can, we are told to talk to the child in the womb. As you are talking to the child in the womb, this prepare you to talk for the next eighteen years. Challenging, challenging and more challenging is parenting. No one, no, no one has the *perfect parent or answer to the process.*

There is a process going with the doctors who excel in genetic structuring with the eggs of smart persons being harvested with other smart persons to create a perfect embryo. Oh, well. The average parent can not afford that process anyway….; and this has not been proven.

Let us take a good hard look at the old-fashioned method of parenting: with a belt or other physical forms of punishments. Get the handcuffs ready for you will be arrested, for child abuse. We are living in a world where there is sometimes no rhyme nor reason, for the situation at hand. Love will have to lead the way for the path of love leads to a positive solution to many problems with our children. Narcissism seems too be a growing negative in parenting today. There is a vast advent of youth who have regards just to themselves, without consideration for others. Their minds become criminal and lacking compassion. Parenting a child who have or project this mindset is super complex and requires professional therapy. Most parents know what their child can do, be it good or bad.

Caring, Caring, Caring

Parenting by Example

MENTORS ARE

★

Unselfish
Believing
Inspiring
Overwhelming
Relentless
Futuristic
Un-abrasive
Unifying
Protective
Constraining
Exemplifying
Containing

Parenting by Example

Parenting by example, with love in the mix, exemplifies and defines who we are as parents. Having a sincere and serious approach to our children's concerns and needs creates a path of instinctive wisdom that cannot be denied. Building trust with a child is especially difficult during the puberty years, because of the high regard that they have for their friends. This alone creates a case scenario – when they choose the wrong friends. Consistency in parenting is needed; it is the gateway to good habits. Good habits are formed by doing positive and good things with the children, on a regular basis. Covert and questionable practices on the part of the parent leads the child to distrust and insecurities.

Maintaining a 'you can talk to me about anything' relationship with your children takes a good deal of hard work on the part of the parent. Remember, children do mimic their parents, in some cases.

Cultivating the child to be the best they can be in school or in any challenging situation is not an easy pursuit. You must, as a parent, know where each child's strengths lie. It does not matter if some of the child's abilities are not distinguishable, some way or another it is up to the parent to develop positive attributes. Remember, sometimes people can say so many negative things about a child that they start to believe it. It works both ways; in parenting you repeat so many positive things to the child they become confident and secure.

Reaching for the stars should always be there in actions, demeanors and mindset of children who are motivated by their parents. Self-regard culminating with self-respect relates to the parenting of bygone years, but certainly can be applicable in today's (*anything goes*) world. Character is not old-fashioned and teaching a child to be an individual is worthwhile pursuit.

Is there any such thing as perfect parenting? The question asked, a variety of answers are given.

Tolerance of other people's race, creed, color, different cultures, should be a part of positive parenting. Tolerance helps us to respond when a child tells a parent that the other religion – Muslim, Hindu, Buddhism, or the many forms of worship – appeals to them rather than the family traditional way of worship, Protestant or Catholic sect.

While being blatant that parenting is not a bowl of sweet, delicious cherries, let us refer to the single parent with two children, recently divorced, who must earn a living for food and shelter. This parent has a court battle for full custody of the children; or another option of working. One cannot go to court and work at the same time.

The answer to this problem, and many other parenting complexities is not easy. As we pass the baton of parenting on to our children. As we as grandparents see them making some of the same blunders and mistakes that we made, let us remember that we are human and that human errors are going to be made.

The impact of the human spirit is alive and well. The human spirit is manufactured and maintained by God. The human spirit is undefeatable because the great God that we serve levels the odds into fervent blessings, and those who recognize these blessings pass them on to others so that they can be blessed also. The God given human spirit is awesome. Parenting is a complex and blessed circumstance all rolled up into one. When God is in it, it is a *"win-win"* situation.

We must remain humble, diligent, and maintain an open-minded approach while striving to be the parent that will feel rewarded by our children's achievements and accomplishments. When the direct opposite occurs, we must also be receptive, understanding and willing to be open-minded in finding a solution.

Who do we pay tribute to in the complex and great world of parenting? Tough question? Yes, it is, I believe that if President Barack Obama's mother was alive today, that she could give us some very valuable information. The finished product is the greatest President of all time with diplomacy, elegance, and intellect all rolled up into one, with the integrity and wisdom to wed the beautiful Michelle, beautiful inside and out.

We look forward to tomorrow as parent, grandparent, foster-parent, forever-parent with the greatest of love, hope, and expectations; with the grandest of aspirations, motivations rooting out all negatives and turning them into positive posturing.

Yes, we are one nation under God indivisible, with liberty and justice "FOR ALL" in parenting and in all aspects, in this great country of America.

Yes, it does take a village to raise a child, a city and a nation.

Thank you for the reading.

Ruth Thacker Fant

Honorary Dedication

Moses Marcus Fant

Caring, Caring, Caring

Honorary Dedication

Richard Fant

Caring, Caring, Caring

Honorary Dedication

Margaret Fant Thacker

Caring, Caring, Caring

Honorary Dedication

Fant, Byrd, Burton Family Reunion

Tribute

Ministers of the Fant, Byrd, Burton Family (23)

About the Author

My rearing, from birth to the age of seventeen, was in a small southern town in South Carolina, with one traffic light in the entire town. After high school graduation in 1955 I became a part of the great migration to northern cities.

My Mom was and still is my hero. She has been deceased for 35 years. I cried for three days when she departed. My Mom's inspiration and contribution to my talents was overwhelming.

She said to me one day, "God has given you many talents; you sing, you speak, you write, but you talk too much. Maybe one day you will use that mouth to become a preacher." It came into fruition. My Mom was awesome.

My middle brother (and I am a middle sister), always challenged me. That is how I became a tomboy. I could outpunch him and climb a tree when he was at the top.

My sister was quiet and very ladylike. I was the direct opposite. My sister came into the world a grown woman. We both love the Lord. She is a Missionary and Sunday School Teacher.

My first round of love produced two children; a smart and talented son, and a beautiful and extremely talented songstress daughter. She gave me two amazing and intelligent grandsons who have chosen outstanding and amazing young women to wed. Wedding bells will soon be ringing.

My second round of love was to a wonderful, wonderful man who gave me 32 years of happiness and love sharing experience. All persons loved him. To know him was to love him.

My third round of love was a boomerang. He was my first love and it is a childhood sweetheart experience coming back around again. He is a wonderful person.

My work endeavors were as Avon Manager; Beautician, Cosmetologist and Beauty Shop Owner; Supervisor of Clerks, and District Manager for World Book Encyclopedia (a most positive experience.) I was the first woman on an all male sales force, and the first high school Home and School President that gave monetary rewards to students who brought failing grades up to passing grades.

I was also an Evangelist receiving twelve evangelistic certificates in a church setting (such an enjoyable experience.)

My formal education is in Christian Theology; Bachelors, Masters and Doctorate. My favorite title is Evangelist as it is most meaningful.

My most enjoyable and gratifying experience was foster parenting these incredible and unfortunate children.

God has blessed me so very enormously. As He continues to bless I pray that He will help me pass those blessings on to others.

Ruth Thacker Fant

Ms. Ruth's

Amazing & Awesome

Celebrity Superlatives

Persons who Exhibit Generosity, Love and Excellence of the Human Spirit in this Great Country of America

★ **President Barack Obama**: *Exemplifying excellence and enormous humanity - awesome president.*

★ **Michelle Obama:** *Intelligent and beautiful, Amazing First Lady.*

★ **Joe Biden:** *Love personified in every way; natural undisguised love for family and country. America needs your integrity.*

★ **Oprah Winfrey:** *Capable, super caring, amazing understanding of people and persons — awesome.*

★ **Gail King:** *Smart, informative, witty, infectious and personable. Amazing amazing.*

★ **Tyler Perry:** *Talented to the core, smart, sensitive and giving — amazing.*

★ **Ellen DeGeneres:** *A living, walking breath of humanity; caring, funny, and sharing — awesome.*

★ **Steve Harvey:** *Revealing the characteristics of the male gender to the benefit of the female population — thank you Steve. Keep on smiling with that million dollar smile — awesome.*

Accolades of Love

Woodrow and Annie, who gave the world the most loving and unselfish man who walked this planet called earth: *Full of love.*

Evangelist LaNaye Cannon: *Bible inspired and full of love.*

Rev. Deborah Griffin-Scott: *God-filled and amazing.* **James and Jeremy**: *Awesome and amazing grandsons – love love love.*

Missionary Mary E. Burnside: *Outstanding.* **My Brothers** in New York, **Odell and George**: *Love, love.*
Angie Caldwell: *Awesome plus awesome.*
George and Jeffrey Caldwell: *Brightest lights in the universe.*
Erica: *Amazing plus amazing.*

Marcus, Dennis, Larry, Earl and Mother Ruth: *Outstanding stars of the Fant family. Shine on and on.* **Spouses:** *Love love.*

Gerald, Julia, Maggie, Tomasina, Juanita, George Richard: *Special love love.*

Mrs. Gail Prater: *Amazing super parent.* **Nia and Keith**: *Outstanding.*

Elder Larry and Gloria Burnside: *In Christ.*

Gay and Nathaniel Thomas: *Super amazing cousins.*

Dr. Clarissa Fant-Gaffney: *Awesome.*

Rev. Dr. Fran Bolton: *Amazing and awesome.*

Congratulations Gloria (GA): *Every happiness.*

Nurse Barb: *Love personified in every way, love love love.*

Rev. Lester Fant, Margie and family: *Love love.*

Vera, dedicated mother to Faith, Vicki, Paula, and Howard: *Love love.*

Velma, Donna, Tiffany and Veronica: *Amazing love.*

Phyllis, Alice and son: *Love love.*

Ms. Trini Rice: *Awesome.*

Joyce Fant Murphy: *Beautiful in Christ.*

Dennis, Derrick, Daryl and Charmain: *In Christ and Amazing.*

Andrea: *Amazing in Special Education.*

Joe, Michelle and Jordan: *Love love love.*

Kathy Fant: best reunion book ever: *Amazing and Incredible.*

Jessica and Dominique: *Awesome and amazing.*

Tarik, Rhonda, Cory, Samara, and Sharif, Sarah and sons: Love, love, love.

The Harris Family: **Marianne**: *Loving and courageous, full of faith. Plus* **Corinthia and Darlene**.

First Lady Lillian Bell: *Above and beyond the call of duty.*

Dr. Dawn: *God filled.* **Christy and Chastity:** *Amazing.*

My Nieces in New York, Jersey City, South Carolina, and Connecticut: *Greatest love.*
Margaret and Valerie: *Super amazing.*
Stephany (big and little), NY and NJ: *Amazing.*

My Nephews in Connecticut, New York, South Carolina: *Love, love.*

My Cousins in North Carolina, Florida, Georgia, Philadelphia, Maryland, Pittsburgh, Ohio: *Super love.*
Joanne, Scarlet and Kelly, Lorraine, Charlie and Anita: *Amazing.*

Roslyn and son Vaughn: *Amazing scriptural readers.*

My 60 yr. friend Shirley Robin and son Hannibal: *Outstanding.*

More 60 yr. friends; Carol, Geneva: *Amazing.*

My World Book Friends: **Claudia**: *You are still a winner*. **Lorine, Celeste**: *Super winners*. **Olie and Gwen**: *Amazing*.

Ms. Deborah Johnson-Clinkscales: *Smart and outstanding*.

My childhood friends Ethel, Mary, Maxine, Sarah, Jessie and Dorothy: *full of fun*. **My childhood cousins Vera and Velma**: *Outstanding*.

My Christian friends Cheryl, Jeanette, Mona, Sylvia, Mary, Barb, Pat, Nora, Francine; and my 61 yr. Christian friend Bertha Childs: *Awesome*.

Rev. Lillian Brand, First Lady: *Most amazing*. **And daughter S. Williams, First Lady**: *Outstanding*

Zion: *Reach for the stars and you can be super blessed by the Creator of the Universe.*

Debra*: Amazing mother.* **Grandmother Jessie***: Love love.*

My ministerial friends at Deliverance Evangelistic Church*: Awesome.*

Joyce, Dennis, Kathy, Mark, Wendy, Dior, Nikki, Shelly, Keith and Sandy, and Saddiq (the amazing genius)*: Much loved.*

My Olive Grove Baptist Church friends: First Lady Eleanor Brown, daughter Norma Vinson, son Brooks Perkins*: Love love love.*

Missionary Earl Smith, daughter Delphine, granddaughter Ashley and great-granddaughter Kremora.*: Love love love*

A CHILD IS AMAZING

★

A child's laughter can make
an angel sing.
A child's innocence creates an
aura of wisdom.
A child's smile can warm the
heart beyond measure.
A child's hands are the
potential artists of the world.
A child's hope can illuminate
the Promise of God.
A child's strength can move
the highest mountain.
A child's love can create the
most beautiful universe.

A child's concept can put an
adult on notice.

A child's peace can be found
in a sea of turmoil.

A child's understanding can
be the anchor for a large ship.

A child's talents and gifts
show they are given by God.

A child's tolerance can be
magical.

A child's wisdom is an
unbelievable protection.

A child's resilience transcends
understanding.

A child's silence suggests
intelligence.

FOSTER PARENTS ARE

Understanding

Loving

Believing

Inspiring

Aspiring

Uplifting

Consistent

Protective

Thoughtful

Dependable

GRANDPARENTS (rearing grandchildren) ARE

★

Super - Grand

Super - Patient

Super - Persevering

Super - Wise

Super - Forgiving

Super - Loving

Super - Problem Solving

Super - Exuberant

Super - Exceptional

Super - Generous

Super - !Blessed!

.

FOREVER PARENTS ARE

Caring

Sharing

Exceptional

Thoughtful

Maintaining

Attaining

Mentoring

Astounding

Encouraging

Complimenting

Implementing

MENTORS ARE

Unselfish

Believing

Inspiring

Overwhelming

Relentless

Futuristic

Un-abrasive

Unifying

Protective

Constraining

Exemplifying

Containing

Notes

Made in the USA
Middletown, DE
14 July 2020